THIS JOURNAL BELONGS TO:

_____

AUTISM JOURNAL WORKBOOK

MY CHILD'S GOALS

SPEECH & COMMUNICATION GOALS

SOCIAL SKILLS GOALS

SENSORY GOALS

ACTIVITY IDEAS

FINE MOTOR ACTIVITIES

VESTIBULAR/PROPRIOCEPTIVE

TACTILE

VISUAL

AUDITORY

ORAL

NOTES:

MILESTONE TRACKER

DATE:

BOOKS TO READ TOGETHER

BOOK TITLE	✓	BOOK TITLE	✓

WEEK 1 ACTIVITIES:

MONDAY

TUESDAY

WEDNESDAY

THURSDAY

FRIDAY

SATURDAY

SUNDAY

WEEK 1:

WEEK OF: _____

SPEECH & COMMUNICATION

SENSORY & O.T.

VESTIBULAR

TACTILE

ORAL MOTOR

MON

TUE

WED

THUR

FRI

SAT

SUN

WEEK 1:

FINE MOTOR

VISUAL

AUDITORY

THIS WEEK'S CHALLENGES

THIS WEEK'S HIGHLIGHTS

SOCIAL SKILLS

OUR FAVORITE MOMENT

WEEKLY APPOINTMENTS

WEEK OF: _____

MON

TUE

WED

THU

WEEKLY APPOINTMENTS

WEEK OF: _____

FRI

_____

_____

_____

_____

_____

SAT

_____

_____

_____

_____

_____

SUN

_____

_____

_____

_____

_____

NOTES:

WEEKLY REFLECTION

Weekly Challenges

Weekly Accomplishments

Favorite Moment of the Week

NOTES

WEEK 2 ACTIVITIES:

MONDAY

TUESDAY

WEDNESDAY

THURSDAY

FRIDAY

SATURDAY

SUNDAY

WEEK 2:

WEEK OF: _____

SPEECH & COMMUNICATION

SENSORY & O.T.

VESTIBULAR

TACTILE

ORAL MOTOR

MON

TUE

WED

THUR

FRI

SAT

SUN

WEEK 2:

TRACKER

FINE MOTOR

VISUAL

AUDITORY

THIS WEEK'S CHALLENGES

SOCIAL SKILLS

THIS WEEK'S HIGHLIGHTS

OUR FAVORITE MOMENT

WEEKLY APPOINTMENTS

WEEK OF: _____

MON

_____

_____

_____

_____

_____

TUE

_____

_____

_____

_____

_____

WED

_____

_____

_____

_____

_____

THU

_____

_____

_____

_____

_____

WEEKLY APPOINTMENTS

WEEK OF: _____

FRI

_____
_____
_____
_____
_____

SAT

_____
_____
_____
_____
_____

SUN

_____
_____
_____
_____
_____

NOTES:

WEEKLY REFLECTION

Weekly Challenges

Weekly Accomplishments

Favorite Moment of the Week

NOTES

WEEK 3 ACTIVITIES:

MONDAY

TUESDAY

WEDNESDAY

THURSDAY

FRIDAY

SATURDAY

SUNDAY

WEEK 3:

WEEK OF: _____

SPEECH & COMMUNICATION

SENSORY & O.T.

VESTIBULAR

TACTILE

ORAL MOTOR

MON

TUE

WED

THUR

FRI

SAT

SUN

WEEK 3:

FINE MOTOR

VISUAL

AUDITORY

THIS WEEK'S CHALLENGES

THIS WEEK'S HIGHLIGHTS

SOCIAL SKILLS

OUR FAVORITE MOMENT

WEEKLY APPOINTMENTS

WEEK OF: _____

MON

TUE

WED

THU

WEEKLY APPOINTMENTS

WEEK OF: _____

FRI

_____
_____
_____
_____
_____

SAT

_____
_____
_____
_____
_____

SUN

_____
_____
_____
_____
_____

NOTES:

WEEKLY REFLECTION

Weekly Challenges

Weekly Accomplishments

Favorite Moment of the Week

NOTES

WEEK 4 ACTIVITIES:

MONDAY

TUESDAY

WEDNESDAY

THURSDAY

FRIDAY

SATURDAY

SUNDAY

WEEK 4:

WEEK OF: _____

SPEECH & COMMUNICATION

SENSORY & O.T.

VESTIBULAR

TACTILE

ORAL MOTOR

MON

TUE

WED

THUR

FRI

SAT

SUN

WEEK 4:

GOALS & PROGRESS
TRACKER

FINE MOTOR

VISUAL

AUDITORY

THIS WEEK'S CHALLENGES

SOCIAL SKILLS

THIS WEEK'S HIGHLIGHTS

OUR FAVORITE MOMENT

WEEKLY APPOINTMENTS

WEEK OF: _____

MON

_____
_____
_____
_____
_____

TUE

_____
_____
_____
_____
_____

WED

_____
_____
_____
_____
_____

THU

_____
_____
_____
_____

WEEKLY APPOINTMENTS

WEEK OF: _____

FRI

SAT

SUN

NOTES:

WEEKLY REFLECTION

Weekly Challenges

Weekly Accomplishments

Favorite Moment of the Week

NOTES

WEEK 5 ACTIVITIES:

MONDAY

TUESDAY

WEDNESDAY

THURSDAY

FRIDAY

SATURDAY

SUNDAY

WEEK 5:

WEEK OF: _____

SPEECH & COMMUNICATION

SENSORY & O.T.

VESTIBULAR

TACTILE

ORAL MOTOR

MON

TUE

WED

THUR

FRI

SAT

SUN

WEEK 5:

FINE MOTOR

VISUAL

AUDITORY

THIS WEEK'S CHALLENGES

THIS WEEK'S HIGHLIGHTS

SOCIAL SKILLS

OUR FAVORITE MOMENT

WEEKLY APPOINTMENTS

WEEK OF: _____

MON

TUE

WED

THU

WEEKLY APPOINTMENTS

WEEK OF: _____

FRI

_____
_____
_____
_____
_____

SAT

_____
_____
_____
_____
_____

SUN

_____
_____
_____
_____
_____

NOTES:

WEEKLY REFLECTION

Weekly Challenges

Weekly Accomplishments

Favorite Moment of the Week

NOTES

WEEK 6 ACTIVITIES:

MONDAY

TUESDAY

WEDNESDAY

THURSDAY

FRIDAY

SATURDAY

SUNDAY

WEEK 6:

WEEK OF: _____

SPEECH & COMMUNICATION

SENSORY & O.T.

VESTIBULAR

TACTILE

ORAL MOTOR

MON

TUE

WED

THUR

FRI

SAT

SUN

WEEK 6:

FINE MOTOR

VISUAL

AUDITORY

THIS WEEK'S CHALLENGES

SOCIAL SKILLS

THIS WEEK'S HIGHLIGHTS

OUR FAVORITE MOMENT

WEEKLY APPOINTMENTS

WEEK OF: _____

MON

TUE

WED

THU

WEEKLY APPOINTMENTS

WEEK OF: _____

FRI

_____
_____
_____
_____
_____

SAT

_____
_____
_____
_____
_____

SUN

_____
_____
_____
_____
_____

NOTES:

WEEKLY REFLECTION

_____
_____
_____
_____
_____
_____
_____
_____
_____
_____
_____
_____
_____
_____
_____
_____

Weekly Challenges

Weekly Accomplishments

Favorite Moment of the Week

NOTES

WEEK 7 ACTIVITIES:

MONDAY

TUESDAY

WEDNESDAY

THURSDAY

FRIDAY

SATURDAY

SUNDAY

WEEK 7:

WEEK OF: _____

SPEECH & COMMUNICATION

SENSORY & O.T.

VESTIBULAR

TACTILE

ORAL MOTOR

MON

TUE

WED

THUR

FRI

SAT

SUN

WEEK 7:

FINE MOTOR

VISUAL

AUDITORY

THIS WEEK'S CHALLENGES

SOCIAL SKILLS

THIS WEEK'S HIGHLIGHTS

OUR FAVORITE MOMENT

WEEKLY APPOINTMENTS

WEEK OF: _____

MON

_____
_____
_____
_____
_____

TUE

_____
_____
_____
_____
_____

WED

_____
_____
_____
_____
_____

THU

_____
_____
_____
_____
_____

WEEKLY APPOINTMENTS

WEEK OF: _____

FRI

_____
_____
_____
_____
_____

SAT

_____
_____
_____
_____
_____
_____

SUN

_____
_____
_____
_____
_____

NOTES:

WEEKLY REFLECTION

Weekly Challenges

Weekly Accomplishments

Favorite Moment of the Week

NOTES

WEEK 8 ACTIVITIES:

MONDAY

TUESDAY

WEDNESDAY

THURSDAY

FRIDAY

SATURDAY

SUNDAY

WEEK 8:

WEEK OF: _____

SPEECH & COMMUNICATION

SENSORY & O.T.

VESTIBULAR

TACTILE

ORAL MOTOR

MON

TUE

WED

THUR

FRI

SAT

SUN

WEEK 8:

FINE MOTOR

VISUAL

AUDITORY

THIS WEEK'S CHALLENGES

SOCIAL SKILLS

THIS WEEK'S HIGHLIGHTS

OUR FAVORITE MOMENT

WEEKLY APPOINTMENTS

WEEK OF: _____

MON

_____
_____
_____
_____
_____

TUE

_____
_____
_____
_____
_____

WED

_____
_____
_____
_____
_____

THU

_____
_____
_____
_____
_____

WEEKLY APPOINTMENTS

WEEK OF: _____

FRI	
	_____
	_____
	_____
	_____

SAT	
	_____
	_____
	_____
	_____

SUN	
	_____
	_____
	_____
	_____

NOTES:

WEEKLY REFLECTION

Weekly Challenges

Weekly Accomplishments

Favorite Moment of the Week

NOTES

WEEK 9 ACTIVITIES:

MONDAY

TUESDAY

WEDNESDAY

THURSDAY

FRIDAY

SATURDAY

SUNDAY

WEEK 9:

WEEK OF: _____

SPEECH & COMMUNICATION

SENSORY & O.T.

VESTIBULAR

TACTILE

ORAL MOTOR

MON

TUE

WED

THUR

FRI

SAT

SUN

WEEK 9:

FINE MOTOR

VISUAL

AUDITORY

THIS WEEK'S CHALLENGES

THIS WEEK'S HIGHLIGHTS

SOCIAL SKILLS

OUR FAVORITE MOMENT

WEEKLY APPOINTMENTS

WEEK OF: _____

MON

_____
_____
_____
_____
_____

TUE

_____
_____
_____
_____
_____

WED

_____
_____
_____
_____
_____

THU

_____
_____
_____
_____
_____

WEEKLY APPOINTMENTS

WEEK OF: _____

FRI

_____

_____

_____

_____

_____

SAT

_____

_____

_____

_____

_____

SUN

_____

_____

_____

_____

_____

NOTES:

WEEKLY REFLECTION

Weekly Challenges

Weekly Accomplishments

Favorite Moment of the Week

NOTES

WEEK 10 ACTIVITIES:

MONDAY

TUESDAY

WEDNESDAY

THURSDAY

FRIDAY

SATURDAY

SUNDAY

WEEK 10:

WEEK OF: _____

SPEECH & COMMUNICATION

SENSORY & O.T.

VESTIBULAR

TACTILE

ORAL MOTOR

MON

TUE

WED

THUR

FRI

SAT

SUN

WEEK 10:

FINE MOTOR

VISUAL

AUDITORY

THIS WEEK'S CHALLENGES

THIS WEEK'S HIGHLIGHTS

SOCIAL SKILLS

OUR FAVORITE MOMENT

WEEKLY APPOINTMENTS

WEEK OF: _____

MON

TUE

WED

THU

WEEKLY APPOINTMENTS

WEEK OF: _____

FRI

_____
_____
_____
_____
_____

SAT

_____
_____
_____
_____
_____

SUN

_____
_____
_____
_____
_____

NOTES:

WEEKLY REFLECTION

Weekly Challenges

Weekly Accomplishments

Favorite Moment of the Week

NOTES

WEEK 11 ACTIVITIES:

MONDAY

TUESDAY

WEDNESDAY

THURSDAY

FRIDAY

SATURDAY

SUNDAY

WEEK 11:

WEEK OF: _____

SPEECH & COMMUNICATION

SENSORY & O.T.

VESTIBULAR

TACTILE

ORAL MOTOR

MON

TUE

WED

THUR

FRI

SAT

SUN

WEEK 11:

FINE MOTOR

VISUAL

AUDITORY

THIS WEEK'S CHALLENGES

THIS WEEK'S HIGHLIGHTS

SOCIAL SKILLS

OUR FAVORITE MOMENT

WEEKLY APPOINTMENTS

WEEK OF: _____

MON

TUE

WED

THU

WEEKLY APPOINTMENTS

WEEK OF: _____

FRI

_____
_____
_____
_____
_____

SAT

_____
_____
_____
_____
_____

SUN

_____
_____
_____
_____
_____

NOTES:

WEEKLY REFLECTION

Weekly Challenges

Weekly Accomplishments

Favorite Moment of the Week

NOTES

WEEK 12 ACTIVITIES:

MONDAY

TUESDAY

WEDNESDAY

THURSDAY

FRIDAY

SATURDAY

SUNDAY

WEEK 12:

WEEK OF: _____

SPEECH & COMMUNICATION

SENSORY & O.T.

VESTIBULAR

TACTILE

ORAL MOTOR

MON

TUE

WED

THUR

FRI

SAT

SUN

WEEK 12:

FINE MOTOR

VISUAL

AUDITORY

THIS WEEK'S CHALLENGES

SOCIAL SKILLS

THIS WEEK'S HIGHLIGHTS

OUR FAVORITE MOMENT

WEEKLY APPOINTMENTS

WEEK OF: _____

MON

_____

_____

_____

_____

_____

TUE

_____

_____

_____

_____

_____

WED

_____

_____

_____

_____

_____

THU

_____

_____

_____

_____

_____

WEEKLY APPOINTMENTS

WEEK OF: _____

FRI

_____
_____
_____
_____
_____

SAT

_____
_____
_____
_____
_____

SUN

_____
_____
_____
_____
_____

NOTES:

WEEKLY REFLECTION

Weekly Challenges

Weekly Accomplishments

Favorite Moment of the Week

NOTES

WEEK 13 ACTIVITIES:

MONDAY

TUESDAY

WEDNESDAY

THURSDAY

FRIDAY

SATURDAY

SUNDAY

WEEK 13:

WEEK OF: _____

SPEECH & COMMUNICATION

SENSORY & O.T.

VESTIBULAR

TACTILE

ORAL MOTOR

MON

TUE

WED

THUR

FRI

SAT

SUN

WEEK 13:

FINE MOTOR

VISUAL

AUDITORY

THIS WEEK'S CHALLENGES

THIS WEEK'S HIGHLIGHTS

SOCIAL SKILLS

OUR FAVORITE MOMENT

WEEKLY APPOINTMENTS

WEEK OF: _____

MON

TUE

WED

THU

WEEKLY APPOINTMENTS

WEEK OF: _____

FRI

_____
_____
_____
_____
_____

SAT

_____
_____
_____
_____
_____

SUN

_____
_____
_____
_____
_____

NOTES:

WEEKLY REFLECTION

_____
_____
_____
_____
_____
_____
_____
_____
_____
_____
_____
_____
_____
_____
_____
_____
_____
_____
_____

Weekly Challenges

Weekly Accomplishments

Favorite Moment of the Week

NOTES

WEEK 14 ACTIVITIES:

MONDAY

TUESDAY

WEDNESDAY

THURSDAY

FRIDAY

SATURDAY

SUNDAY

WEEK 14:

WEEK OF: _____

SPEECH & COMMUNICATION

SENSORY & O.T.

VESTIBULAR

TACTILE

ORAL MOTOR

MON

TUE

WED

THUR

FRI

SAT

SUN

WEEK 14:

FINE MOTOR

VISUAL

AUDITORY

THIS WEEK'S CHALLENGES

THIS WEEK'S HIGHLIGHTS

SOCIAL SKILLS

OUR FAVORITE MOMENT

WEEKLY APPOINTMENTS

WEEK OF: _____

MON

_____
_____
_____
_____
_____

TUE

_____
_____
_____
_____
_____

WED

_____
_____
_____
_____
_____

THU

_____
_____
_____
_____
_____

WEEKLY APPOINTMENTS

WEEK OF: _____

FRI

_____
_____
_____
_____
_____

SAT

_____
_____
_____
_____
_____

SUN

_____
_____
_____
_____
_____

NOTES:

WEEKLY REFLECTION

Weekly Challenges

Weekly Accomplishments

Favorite Moment of the Week

NOTES

WEEK 15 ACTIVITIES:

MONDAY

TUESDAY

WEDNESDAY

THURSDAY

FRIDAY

SATURDAY

SUNDAY

WEEK 15:

WEEK OF: _____

SPEECH & COMMUNICATION

SENSORY & O.T.

VESTIBULAR

TACTILE

ORAL MOTOR

MON

TUE

WED

THUR

FRI

SAT

SUN

WEEK 15:

FINE MOTOR

VISUAL

AUDITORY

THIS WEEK'S CHALLENGES

SOCIAL SKILLS

THIS WEEK'S HIGHLIGHTS

OUR FAVORITE MOMENT

WEEKLY APPOINTMENTS

WEEK OF: _____

MON

TUE

WED

THU

WEEKLY APPOINTMENTS

WEEK OF: _____

FRI

_____
_____
_____
_____
_____

SAT

_____
_____
_____
_____
_____

SUN

_____
_____
_____
_____
_____

NOTES:

WEEKLY REFLECTION

Weekly Challenges

Weekly Accomplishments

Favorite Moment of the Week

NOTES

WEEK 16 ACTIVITIES:

MONDAY

TUESDAY

WEDNESDAY

THURSDAY

FRIDAY

SATURDAY

SUNDAY

WEEK 16:

WEEK OF: _____

SPEECH & COMMUNICATION

SENSORY & O.T.

VESTIBULAR

TACTILE

ORAL MOTOR

MON

TUE

WED

THUR

FRI

SAT

SUN

WEEK 16:

FINE MOTOR

VISUAL

AUDITORY

THIS WEEK'S CHALLENGES

THIS WEEK'S HIGHLIGHTS

SOCIAL SKILLS

OUR FAVORITE MOMENT

WEEKLY APPOINTMENTS

WEEK OF: _____

MON

TUE

WED

THU

WEEKLY APPOINTMENTS

WEEK OF: _____

FRI

_____
_____
_____
_____
_____

SAT

_____
_____
_____
_____
_____

SUN

_____
_____
_____
_____
_____

NOTES:

WEEKLY REFLECTION

Weekly Challenges

Weekly Accomplishments

Favorite Moment of the Week

NOTES

WEEK 17 ACTIVITIES:

MONDAY

TUESDAY

WEDNESDAY

THURSDAY

FRIDAY

SATURDAY

SUNDAY

WEEK 17:

WEEK OF: _____

SPEECH & COMMUNICATION

SENSORY & O.T.

VESTIBULAR

TACTILE

ORAL MOTOR

MON

TUE

WED

THUR

FRI

SAT

SUN

WEEK 17:

FINE MOTOR

VISUAL

AUDITORY

THIS WEEK'S CHALLENGES

THIS WEEK'S HIGHLIGHTS

SOCIAL SKILLS

OUR FAVORITE MOMENT

WEEKLY APPOINTMENTS

WEEK OF: _____

MON
_____
_____
_____
_____
_____

TUE
_____
_____
_____
_____
_____

WED
_____
_____
_____
_____
_____

THU
_____
_____
_____
_____
_____

WEEKLY APPOINTMENTS

WEEK OF: _____

FRI

_____
_____
_____
_____
_____

SAT

_____
_____
_____
_____
_____

SUN

_____
_____
_____
_____
_____

NOTES:

WEEKLY REFLECTION

Weekly Challenges

Weekly Accomplishments

Favorite Moment of the Week

NOTES

WEEK 18 ACTIVITIES:

MONDAY

TUESDAY

WEDNESDAY

THURSDAY

FRIDAY

SATURDAY

SUNDAY

WEEK 18:

WEEK OF: _____

SPEECH & COMMUNICATION

SENSORY & O.T.

VESTIBULAR

TACTILE

ORAL MOTOR

MON

TUE

WED

THUR

FRI

SAT

SUN

WEEK 18:

FINE MOTOR

VISUAL

AUDITORY

THIS WEEK'S CHALLENGES

SOCIAL SKILLS

THIS WEEK'S HIGHLIGHTS

OUR FAVORITE MOMENT

WEEKLY APPOINTMENTS

WEEK OF: _____

MON

TUE

WED

THU

WEEKLY APPOINTMENTS

WEEK OF: _____

FRI

_____
_____
_____
_____
_____

SAT

_____
_____
_____
_____
_____

SUN

_____
_____
_____
_____
_____

NOTES:

WEEKLY REFLECTION

Weekly Challenges

Weekly Accomplishments

Favorite Moment of the Week

NOTES

WEEK 19 ACTIVITIES:

MONDAY

TUESDAY

WEDNESDAY

THURSDAY

FRIDAY

SATURDAY

SUNDAY

WEEK 19:

WEEK OF: _____

SPEECH & COMMUNICATION

SENSORY & O.T.

VESTIBULAR

TACTILE

ORAL MOTOR

MON

TUE

WED

THUR

FRI

SAT

SUN

WEEK 19:

FINE MOTOR

VISUAL

AUDITORY

THIS WEEK'S CHALLENGES

SOCIAL SKILLS

THIS WEEK'S HIGHLIGHTS

OUR FAVORITE MOMENT

WEEKLY APPOINTMENTS

WEEK OF: _____

MON

_____
_____
_____
_____
_____

TUE

_____
_____
_____
_____
_____

WED

_____
_____
_____
_____
_____

THU

_____
_____
_____
_____
_____

WEEKLY APPOINTMENTS

WEEK OF: _____

FRI

_____
_____
_____
_____
_____

SAT

_____
_____
_____
_____
_____

SUN

_____
_____
_____
_____

NOTES:

WEEKLY REFLECTION

Weekly Challenges

Weekly Accomplishments

Favorite Moment of the Week

NOTES

WEEK 20 ACTIVITIES:

MONDAY

TUESDAY

WEDNESDAY

THURSDAY

FRIDAY

SATURDAY

SUNDAY

WEEK 20:

WEEK OF: _____

SPEECH & COMMUNICATION

SENSORY & O.T.

VESTIBULAR

TACTILE

ORAL MOTOR

MON

TUE

WED

THUR

FRI

SAT

SUN

WEEK 20:

FINE MOTOR

VISUAL

AUDITORY

THIS WEEK'S CHALLENGES

SOCIAL SKILLS

THIS WEEK'S HIGHLIGHTS

OUR FAVORITE MOMENT

WEEKLY APPOINTMENTS

WEEK OF: _____

MON

TUE

WED

THU

WEEKLY APPOINTMENTS

WEEK OF: _____

FRI

_____
_____
_____
_____
_____

SAT

_____
_____
_____
_____
_____

SUN

_____
_____
_____
_____
_____

NOTES:

WEEKLY REFLECTION

Weekly Challenges

Weekly Accomplishments

Favorite Moment of the Week

NOTES

Made in the USA
Las Vegas, NV
17 June 2021